Azraelle

Angel of Life and Death

Printed in the United Kingdom
First Printing, 2021
ISBN: Print (Hard Cover):
978-1-8383723-1-6

Published by Purple Parrot Publishing
www.purpleparrotpublishing.co.uk

About the Author

Author Deborah Sykes is also the creator and founder of 12millionminds CIC, a mental health service, where she delivers support as an Emotional Health Coach.

Emotional Health Coaching helps clients manage their emotions and understand their behaviours attached to their emotions.

Death of a loved one is one of the biggest traumas that children can experience, and if the whole family are affected by the same trauma, speaking to the children is the hardest part.

Deborah has the privilege of working with amazing families, and children, especially those on the autism spectrum who don't fully understand death in the softer language or shielded way a family may choose to communicate.

Deborah has written this book to explain death and grief using an angel called Azraelle. Through Azraelle she answers the questions that, in her experience, children need answers to.

Dedication

I can still recall every detail of the day Grandad Bob died, as my pet rabbit Pip died on the same day. I felt scared, shocked, worried and confused. The sadness was so great that I wore it like a heavy coat.

I am sure I would have asked my parents question after question, and I dont recall every detail of how they helped me and my 3 brothers understand the impact of trauma and death, but I do remember always feeling safe. Legends. Thank you.

To My Prince Charming Rob, My Faye, Pat & Buck and Our Butler family, I love you all so much.

'Love is the greatest gift of life.'

How to use this book

This book has been written in two parts.

Book One

Azraelle is introduced to our younger readers using language that you can comfortably adopt to help you start your own coversation around death, grief and sadness.

Book Two

Azraelle introduces herself to the passing soul and guides them on their journey through to Eternity.

Simply turn the book over and upside down.

Hello, I am an angel.

My name is **Azraelle**.

I am the angel of life and death.

I have a very important job.
I am a protector of souls

Your soul is the energy
within your body.

Your soul is eternal
– this means it
lives forever.

Before a baby is born,
I protect their soul on the
journey until they arrive
with their parents.

The new parents become the
guardian of the baby's soul.

When the baby is grown up,
they become the guardian of
their own soul until they die.

During death, the soul leaves the body
and travels to a place called Eternity.

Eternity is an endless life after death.

I am there during death and protect
the soul on its journey to Eternity.

If I have visited your family,
someone you love has died,
and I have taken their soul
on its journey to Eternity.

DEATH
IS A HUGE EVENT

Death is such an important part of life.

All living things, plants, animals and people die.

*Death is something so incredibly messy, sad and forever...
there is no return from death.*

People find death and dying very
difficult things to talk about.

They may say things like:

Passed away.

No longer with us.

Lost their life.

Resting in peace.

Lost their battle.

Death happens when the body
can no longer work.

The medical term for death
is 'the end of life'.

All people will experience
death during their life.

Most people do not know
when they will die.

Death can occur for many
reasons: an accident, event
or an illness.

LIZZIE'S WOOD.

Some people get sick and this can damage their body
and make it too weak to carry on living.

Some people die in an accident or tragedy.

Some people choose the day that they die;
this is called suicide.

Suicide means they have chosen
to end their own life.

They do this because their mind has become
overwhelmed and their reason to live
has been lost.

Every death leaves a huge amount of sadness,
sorrow and a feeling of loss for everyone left behind.

There are many feelings linked to death.

Grief, sadness, loneliness, shock, anger, denial,
worry, stress, despair, love, hope or numbness.

If there has been a lot of suffering and pain before death,
then some people may feel relief.

All of these feelings
are real and perfectly
normal.

It is OK to have any of
these feelings.

You may have them for a long
time and that is OK too.

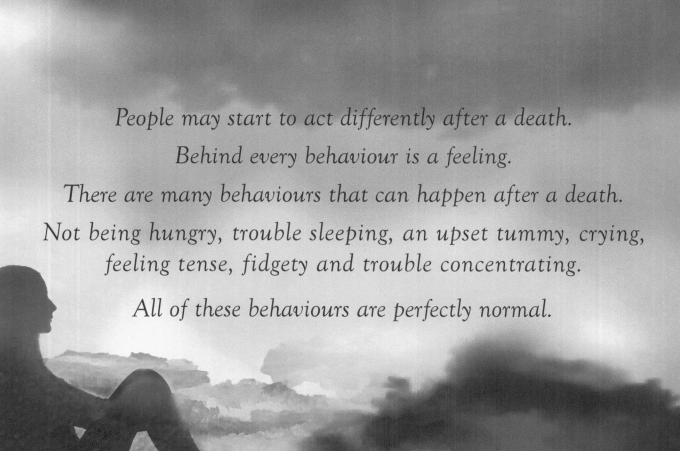

People may start to act differently after a death.

Behind every behaviour is a feeling.

There are many behaviours that can happen after a death.

Not being hungry, trouble sleeping, an upset tummy, crying,
feeling tense, fidgety and trouble concentrating.

All of these behaviours are perfectly normal.

When people have these reactions to death, we say they are grieving.

Grief is a normal feeling, and grieving is a reaction to death and loss.

Grief is horrible.

The feeling of grief is often the strongest straight after death.

Going through grief does not mean we will forget the person who has died.

There are no timescales for how long your grief will last.

Grieving
is a process
that each person will
go through differently;
it is a personal experience.

It is normal to feel the loss
of someone we love forever.

Grief is the price we pay
for love.

It can take a while to accept a death and that the person will not be seen again.

You won't hear their voice or laughter again, and this is so very sad.

It is important to let your sadness out and cry.

Crying helps us on our journey with grief.

It helps us to heal, understand and accept the death.

After a death,
families and friends come
together to comfort each other in their grief.

They are brought together by their huge,
shared love of the person who has died.

It is normal to recall memories and stories
that make them laugh and cry.

It is perfectly OK to laugh and cry.

Family and friends will plan how they want to
celebrate the life of the person who has died.

A burial or a cremation of the person's
body is planned. This is the time for everyone to
say their final goodbye and wish them a
safe journey to Eternity.

How will you remember a loved one?

How will you keep their memory alive?

How will you honour them and make them proud?

We would love to hear your ideas, please email us at:

angelservices@angelic.com.

This is the end of Book One.

*To read Book Two, go to the back cover,
turn the book over and upside down.*

This is the end of Book Two.

To read Book One, go to the front cover,
turn the book over and upside down.

To read Book One, go to the front cover, turn the book over and upside down.

With You Vision TV you will never miss an event your family or friends attend; birthdays, school plays, weddings, anniversaries, football games or ballet classes.

Eternity really is an endless life after death.

You will have your own room in the palace.
Your bed and pillows will be as soft as clouds.
The covers and curtains will be made of the finest, softest silk.
You'll have a lovely comfy sofa and huge chair and a fabulous TV.

This TV is very special. It's called You Vision TV.
You will be able to watch the loved ones that you've left behind.
They will each have their own channel.
You'll be able to watch them as often as you like.

For the younger souls in Eternity,
there are water parks, roller blading,
go-karts and kites too.

There are no schools in Eternity, because, in this place,
having fun with your family and friends forever is an education.

No-one goes to work in Eternity; here you can enjoy your hobbies,
arts and leisure, and learn new things.

Every evening there is music
and dancing in the Grand Hall.

In Eternity you drink the clearest spring water
and when there are celebrations, there is every
colour of fizzy pop to enjoy.

The choice of food in the palace is so big that
it will suit everyone's taste. Once you have settled,
you will be asked for a list of your favourite foods.

At the end of the Grand Hall, there is a selection of cakes,
desserts and over 100 flavours of ice creams to sample
over and over again

You don't need money, cards or banks in Eternity;
you will receive everything you could possibly
need and it is paid for only with love.

The family palace is
so beautiful.

It has many rooms, a Grand Hall
with dining tables that stretch for miles,
grand pianos, chandeliers, dance floors, crystal
glasses, the finest china plates and gold cutlery.

There are also beautiful gardens, terraces, fields
and meadows to walk and run through.

Every sport you can possibly imagine can be
played and watched here. There are swimming
pools, tennis and netball courts and crazy golf,
pitches to play football and cricket, snooker
tables and a horse racing track.

Eternity is full of people you have known on Earth before they died. Your family, old friends and all of your pets are waiting to greet you.

Your family, that arrived in Eternity before you, live in a HUGE floating palace.

Everyone will be excited to see you and will throw a huge party to celebrate your arrival.

To mark your arrival, they will send rainbows, shiny pennies and beautiful white feathers down to Earth through sunbeams.

This lets everyone know that you have arrived safely and that you are happy.

To start our journey to Eternity, we
must first dress you in your favourite clothes
and prepare ourselves to travel.

The portals we use to travel to and from Eternity
are beams of light from the sun or the moon. One is open
and ready just for us.

Eternity is the most amazing place; it is so happy and peaceful.

Your first days will be spent resting and resetting your energy.
I will help you to understand, adjust and accept
your new life in Eternity.

You may be feeling worried,
scared, lost and confused. This is normal.

You are not alone; I am here right beside you and
I feel trusted as your guide.

Your body no longer works, it will remain here on Earth for your
family to say goodbye to and to help them to accept your death.

You are perfectly whole again. The illnesses that your body held
onto as pain and suffering are gone now - forever.

You no longer need your possessions. You can leave your walking
stick, false teeth, slippers, glasses or medicines behind.
You are a travelling soul, so you do not need them.

Your soul is light as a feather and no
longer weighed down.

Please don't be afraid.

I am here to comfort you and protect your soul, as your life here on Earth is about to end.

I am here to hold your hand and guide you on your journey to Eternity.

This is your time to leave.

Hello, I am an angel.

My name is **Azraelle**.

I am the angel of life and death.

Azraelle

Angel *of* Life *and* Death